HASHEM'S LOVE

by Henrietta Charach, MA, OTR

Illustrated by Devorah Weinberg

Hashem's Love
Second Edition
August 2020, Av 5780

ISBN 978-1-61704-151-8

All rights reserved, including the right to reproduce this book or portions thereof, in any form, without prior permission, in writing, from the author.

Printed in the USA

A tribute to my mother's legacy and life
Henrietta Charach
Henya bas Aharon Yosef A"H
Whose Yahrzeit is the 9th of Av

Time moves along like waves
In the ocean of life
In contrast, legacies last forever
My mother's legacy is eternal
Her light is infinitely shining so bright
from above
Perpetually glistening with love
and radiance
We're always linked in the chain of life keeping her spirit alive
via emulating her qualities:
Compassion, benevolence, empathy, soft heartedness...
Yet strength and perseverence through obstacles and uncertainty
With a positive and joyful attitude and song
And through her life story

IY"H we will be reunited with Moshiach immediately
Thank You Hashem (G-d)
Thank you Ma A"H (Mom)

May all of your family perpetuate this
Eternal message of Hashem's Love
Especially in these 9 days of Menachem Av
Hashem is our comfort, our true Father

Love, the Charach and Coates Families

From the heavens above,

Hashem sent us His love

He gave us the grass and the trees

And the beautiful earthsong within the breeze

The flowers in the meadows growing strong

And to the night sky He blessed with a song
He gave us the sea and the oceans below

Even the big mountains covered with snow.

He gave us the seasons
Summer, winter and spring

For in those seasons the birds can sing.

Thank You Hashem
For the day and the night,
For without it there would be
No sun, moon or light.